I0105006

PAR AVION
AIR MAIL
CORREO AEREO

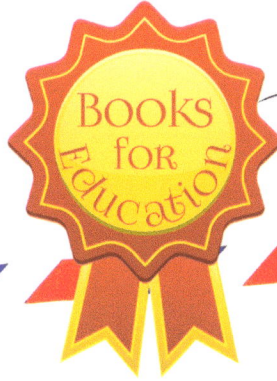

Letter to My Dreams™
for the Children of the World

By
Pilar Vélez

To the visionaries that transform the world
with the greatness of their dreams

To all the children of the planet. No matter where they were born
or where they are, their language, race, color, religion, or gender.
May their love, innocence, and courage inspire an inclusive society that
guarantees their rights and which recognizes - through their
own dreams - the opportunity to transform the world.
For their present. And for the future of humanity.

snow
fountain
press

Scan this code to practice the vocabulary and receive Canguro The Postman's mail.

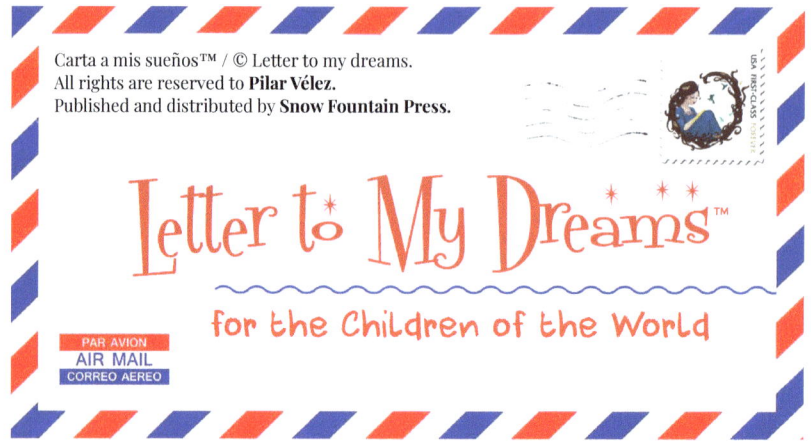

Carta a mis sueños™ / © Letter to my dreams.
All rights are reserved to **Pilar Vélez.**
Published and distributed by **Snow Fountain Press.**

Letter to My Dreams™
for the Children of the World

PAR AVION
AIR MAIL
CORREO AEREO

Spanish Edition, June 2021
Engish Edition, February 2022
©2022, Pilar Vélez
Snow Fountain Press
25 SE 2nd. Avenue, Suite 316 Miami, FL 33131

ISBN: 978-1-957417-04-2

www.lettertomydreams.com
www.pilarvelez.com
www.snowfountainpress.com
Mail to: pilarv@snowfountainpress.com

Illustrated and designed by Alynor Díaz
Translated by Silvia Rafti
Copy editing and proofreading by Nellie Rivera Rentas

Online Platform and workshops promoted by Hispanic Heritage Literature Organization / Milibrohispano.

Letter to My Dreams Books series:
Letter to my Dreams for Planet Earth
Letter to my Dreams for the Children of the World
Letter to my Dreams for Humanity
Letter to my Dreams for the Women of the World
Letter to my Dreams for the Workers of the World

Books are available in English and Spanish.

@cangurothepostman
@snowfountainpress
@pilarvelezzamparelli

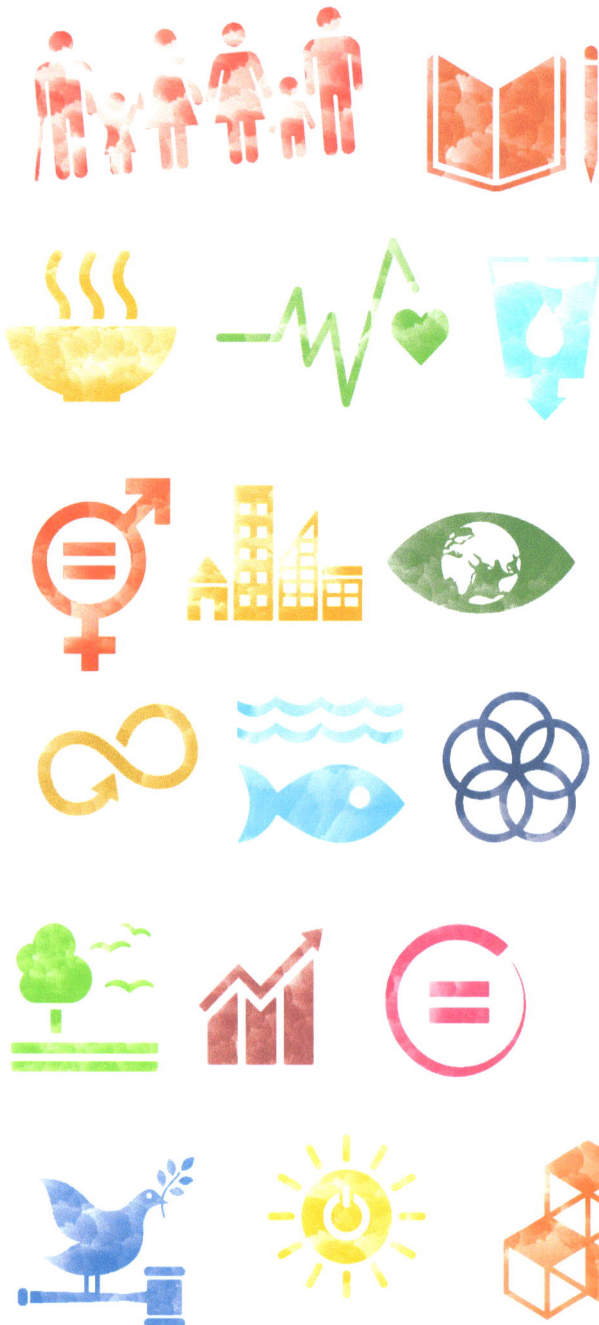

Letter to My Dreams™

Creative reading and writing to inspire children and adolescents. Our leaders of tomorrow.

After publishing *Letter to My Dreams for Planet Earth*, the first volume in the series *Letter to My Dreams*™, —in which we aim to inspire children and adolescents to protect and develop responsible attitudes towards the environment— we are honored to present the second volume: *Letter to My Dreams*™ *for the Children of the World*.

This book presents the life stories of children and young people who have persevered in their dreams and impacted the lives of thousands of people while inspiring others not to give up their ideals. This edition highlights how important it is for our children, adolescents, and the general population to learn about and become familiar with the 17 Sustainable Development Goals proposed by the United Nations (UN). These principles should be the source of inspiration for all of us to work together for a better future.

A large percentage of the world's population is between the ages of 10 and 24. It is imperative to issue a renewing message for them: optimistic and empathetic regarding the world's current problems and the challenges for these new generations.

Aware of this need, we present a collection of biographies and activities that feature relevant issues, following the **17 goals proposed in the 2030 Agenda** by the UN but adapted for easy understanding. The topics presented include peace, justice, poverty, hunger, health, gender equality, the need for energy

¡HI!

I AM CANGURO THE POSTMAN FROM LETTER TO MY DREAMS

resources, drinking water, infrastructure, and the right to work, among other relevant issues.

In addition to raising awareness and contributing to awakening leadership, our methodology stimulates perception, imagination, concentration, acquisition of information, and vocabulary. Likewise, it strengthens oral and writing skills, facilitates interpretation, and encourages analysis and critical thought, individual work, and teamwork.

Letter to My Dreams™ for the Children of the World, like all volumes of *Letter to My Dreams™* is composed of cross-cutting themes that enrich training and connect learning from a humanistic perspective so that children and adolescents act with autonomous values and are aware of the current transformations and those that the future holds for them. We contribute to a sensitive awakening and the need not only to instruct but also to educate human beings respectful of everyone's rights and aware of their duties, with their own values and empowered to forge a society in which peace and human well-being without discrimination prevail.

We are the change we desire!

Pilar Vélez

Let's have fun together!
Today is the most important day of our lives

THEMATIC SUMMARY FOR PARENTS AND TEACHERS

#57 ACTIVITIES

Pedagogical fundamentals of Letter to My Dreams™ for the Children of the World

Comprehensive Education
- Education in population
- Moral and civic education
- Education for peace
- Education for gender equality
- Environmental education

Cross-Sectional Education
- Language
- Environmental Science
- Mathematics
- Social Studies
- Artistic education

Topics
- Procedural
- Conceptual
- Attitudinal

Visit our web page: **www.lettertomydreams.com** and practice the vocabulary from the magical chests of words on our bilingual English/Spanish platform.

THE WORLD HAS A MASTER PLAN

DEAR DREAMER:
We want you to dream and fight for a better world!

Everything we do or fail to do has either a positive or negative impact on the planet and the species that inhabit it. Some dreams cannot wait, and the dream of seeing our world in peace and balance is one of them. If you are a child or a teenager, now is time to talk to you about the critical challenges humanity is facing because, by the time you reach adulthood, it may be too late. We know that you have the strength, wisdom, love, and commitment to make your dreams come true. That is why we want you to also welcome the dream of humanity as your own.

WE PRESENT TO YOU THE MOST IMPORTANT MASTER PLAN OF HUMANITY:
17 GOALS THAT UNITE US AND WE CAN ACCOMPLISH TOGETHER!

In 2012, the United Nations (UN), the most powerful organization on the planet integrated today by 193 countries, gathered its members in Rio de Janeiro, Brazil, with the purpose of unifying criteria and identifying the most urgent universal goals the world needs in environmental, political, and economic matters. That is how the 2030 Agenda was born, containing 17 Sustainable Development Goals (SDGs), making it a master plan for humanity.

¡Learn about the 17 Sustainable Development Goals!

WHY IS SUSTAINABLE DEVELOPMENT IMPORTANT?

Resources are limited; if we do not know how to take care of them and administer them correctly, we will negatively affect the lives of future generations. Sustainable development enables us to meet our current needs without compromising future resources.

Today's citizens are responsible for what we will leave to the next generation.

And we must understand that it is necessary to take actions that cannot be postponed to reverse the damage done to our planet and forge a world committed to life sustainability.

If we do away with resources, we will be leaving a world of poverty and misery to future generations. The world must unite to meet each person's needs and enjoy a better quality of life in conditions of equality, peace, justice, and opportunities.

When we realize that the way we act and think affects others and transcends the future, we will understand that it is necessary to change. It is not enough to acquire knowledge and develop skills. We must also cultivate values and attitudes that contribute to the achievement of our personal goals and contribute to the well-being of humanity. Hence, it is important for all citizens of the world to learn about this master plan of 17 Sustainable Development Goals and do their part. Now is the time to think and act. Each of us has the POWER to change the future by making wise decisions and taking the right actions in the present.

It does not matter where you are or your situation, age, gender, race, economic status, religion, or beliefs: you are a citizen of the world. The planet and what dwells in it make up your home, your present, and your future. Take care of what you have today. Build your dreams and help others build theirs too, turn this mission into your daily "goal." Be inspired by the stories and themes we share in this book. You are fundamental in ensuring that the world has a peaceful and balanced future of well-being, inclusion, and development. Remember: **Do not leave anyone behind!**

Learn more about the 17 goals and ask at school, in your neighborhood, city, and country. How are they contributing?

Our journey through Letter to My Dreams for the Children of the World has started!

BE PART OF THE CHANGE, INSPIRE OTHERS BY EXAMPLE!

The King
Who Could not Dream

O nce upon a time, in a distant country, lived one of the most powerful kings that ever existed. They said he owned so much land that not even he knew how far his kingdom reached and that his wealth was such that his chests of treasures and gold coins could be counted by the hundreds.

The king, who almost nobody knew because he was rarely seen outside palace, spent most of his days strolling through the royal gardens and enjoying lavish parties accompanied by the queen, their three children, the members of the court, and the kings and princes visiting from other kingdoms. But the king, who thought he had it all, was not happy. He lacked an extraordinary thing: he was incapable of dreaming; he could not dream either asleep or awake! He felt envy and even anger when he heard other people talk about their dreams. So one day, full of bitterness, he issued a proclamation by which it was forbidden to dream. And little by little, dreams started disappearing from his kingdom.

Years passed, and one morning when he got up, the king had a strange feeling that he could not understand or explain. He touched his chest and said he felt a a great emptiness squeezing his heart. The queen called the doctor to examine him: the king's heartbeat was normal, the color of his skin was as always, and he had no fever. Without being convinced of evil or the cure, the doctor prepared a syrup with the flower of Goodlife, assuring him that he would be fine after a couple of days of rest and chicken broth.

The king followed the instructions, but it was of no use. As he felt his emptiness getting more prominent, he thought he would feel better with a succulent banquet and a great party. The queen set out to please the king: the musicians and dancers arrived, the courtesans dressed in their best costumes, and turkeys, hams, sweets, and rolls adorned the table. The king ate up until he was full, danced until exhausted, and drank from his favorite wines. At the end of the night, he asked for one of the chests filled with coins to be brought and threw them into the air to celebrate the occasion with a shower of gold. However, despite the fullness in his belly and his flatterers' applauses, the emptiness in his chest was bigger than before.

Overwhelmed and annoyed at not feeling well, he called the magician, who claimed that was a powerful enchantment that could only be cured with his infallible concoction: Star of April. When he drank the potion, the king felt his eyes popping out of their sockets, bulging like a pair of lanterns, and a hurricane wind running through his body and his nose. Unable to avoid it, he released a loud sneeze that lit the fireplace illuminating the palace for a few minutes. The king felt disconsolate and, not knowing why he started crying in front of everyone. Something was missing, but he did not know what. As neither the doctor nor the magician could do anything for him, he commanded the most venerable sage of the kingdom, an older man who lived on the outskirts.

"What do I have? How do I heal from this void?" the king asked despondently.
"Your majesty, there is only one cure for this void: fill it!" answered the old sage.
"And how or with what can you fill something that you do not see and do not know what it is?" exclaimed the king angrily.
"Your Majesty, that emptiness is the lack of a dream," said the sage.
"You ask for something impossible!
No one dreams in this kingdom!" shouted the king arrogantly.

"That would change if the king dreams. Leave your carriage, garments, gold, and knights," the sage continued. "For a day, live with nothing, just like your subjects. Walk the streets and villages, talk to the people, only then will you be cured," concluded the sage.

Having no other choice, the king followed the sage's advice. He dressed as a poor villager and left the palace through a secret passage until he arrived at the first village. He felt afraid and naked, as he had never gone out alone, and he missed his crown and his plush cloak.

He thought someone would recognize him, but no one did. The king walked for several hours and, feeling hungry, he asked a man to give him a loaf of bread, but the man refused and chased him away with a broom. The king felt humiliated and wanted to return to his palace, but he then reconsidered it; if he returned, he would not find the cure to his evil.

He kept walking and noticed the humble houses, the hungry faces, the worn and dirty clothes of the villagers. He stopped at a field where they gave him water to drink. There he saw the elders carrying heavy sacks and barefoot

children plowing the soil under an inclement sun. No one smiled, neither in the field nor the village. Everything was grey as if wrapped in a heavy mist. It was already getting dark, and since the king had not had a bite all day and it was too late to try to return to his palace, he knocked on the door of the last abode he found on the way. In the house lived an old woman and her five grandchildren. The woman opened the door and the king, feeling sorry when he saw the humble hut, asked for something to eat. Speaking in a friendly tone, she invited him to sit down at the table. With no qualms, she took a little soup from each of the dishes she had already served, giving him a generous portion. The king was More so when he saw them holding hands and giving thanks for the food and the day that had ended. At that moment, in that family, he recognized something family something that he did not have: innocence, faith, and courage.

Grateful, the king said goodbye and headed to the forest in search of a place to spend the night. He lit a campfire, laid his head on a log, and, after meditating on the day he had lived, he fell sound asleep.

They say that that night, for perhaps the first time in his long life, the king had a great dream: he saw himself touring his kingdom, dressed in his beautiful red cape, and wearing his crown of gold and rubies on his head. The crowds took to the streets, cheered him on, and threw thousands of flowers at his feet. He saw that all the kingdom's houses were beautiful, and smoke came out of their chimneys. On the tables were loaves of bread, meats, and wines, and people looked happy and healthy. He also saw the children wearing beautiful shoes, playing, and singing. Nothing was missing in his kingdom, everyone was happy, and he saw himself as the most content person on Earth. The emptiness did not exist in his dream.

The night ended, and the king woke up again with those feelings that tore him apart. He knew then that his emptiness was the abandonment of his people and that the cure for his evil was to fulfill that dream and restore harmony and justice.

In all the years of his reign, he had only been occupied with accumulating wealth. He had become a petty and calculating being who was only concerned about his well-being and staying in power.

He returned to his palace without delay, took several chests of gold coins, and gave orders to hire workers, repair houses, and buy food for the people. The queen thought the king had gone mad when they told her that he had also bought flour, bundles of seeds, horses, tools, fabrics, and hides to be distributed among the inhabitants. Frightened, the queen called the court to make him come to his senses because they would be ruined if he continued like this. But the king, instead of listening to them, ordered his tailors, dressmakers, blacksmiths, shoemakers, teachers, and bakers to go to the villages to teach their trades. Finally, he gave instructions to plant trees in all the streets and build plazas and gardens with water fountains, just as he had dreamed.

Soon after, the royal coffers were refilled, as people had multiplied what the king had given them. The realm's cellars were so crammed with grains that he ordered to distribute the excess among other kingdoms. Every time he gave to his people, his heart felt fuller than before. He no longer wanted to be in the palace, but in the villages, with the people. He was happy to listen to them, see them laugh, and share without selfishness. But what he liked most was when the children approached him and hugged him without fear and told him they wanted to be as good as him. And it was that love full of innocence, faith, and courage that genuinely filled his heart and made him immensely happy. His happiness was so generous that he wanted all the people from the kingdom to experience it and have beautiful dreams like the one he had. And so, he abolished the law that prohibited dreaming and established the most important proclamation of his entire life. One that would last until our times: "Only those who have the heart of a child and dare to dream can live in this kingdom."

I have DREAMS

ACTIVITIES

#1 Read the story and write the number of the Sustainable Development Goals addressed in each diamond.

#2

- On a blank page, draw and color the king's dream.
- Imagine your heart and draw it according to this story.
- Write about your most precious treasures.

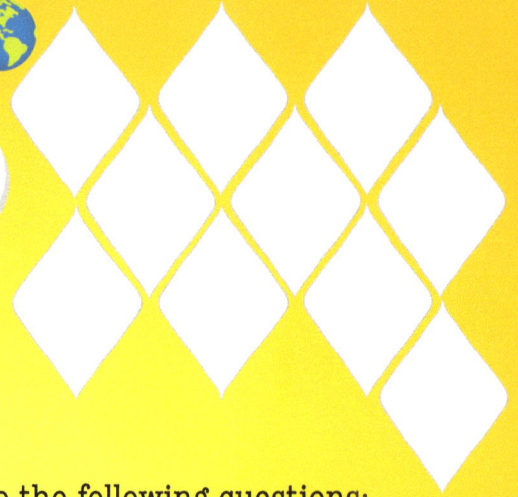

#3

READING COMPREHENSION

Read the story and discuss in a group the answers to the following questions:

- In a few words, what is the story about?
- Why did the king prohibit dreams?
- Do you think the prohibition to dream affected people? How?
- Why did the queen and the court not want the king to give away his treasure?
- How does the king use his treasure after his dream?
- What would have happened if the king had not fulfilled his dream?
- How do you think the king recovered all that he invested?
- What does the king's proclamation mean: "Only those who have the heart of a child and dare to dream can live in this kingdom."
- Several feelings, flaws, and virtues are mentioned in the story. Can you name them?
- What is the moral of the story?

Thinkers' TABLE

#4

- What does it mean to dream?
- What is necessary to make a dream come true?
- Do you think everyone dreams?
- Do you think there are situations where people lose the desire to dream?
- What is the value of a dream?
- What is a treasure, and what is it for?
- Why is it important to cultivate generosity?
- What are the responsibilities of a king or a president?

#5 THINK

- Think about the things you accumulate and do not need
- Do you think you can put them to better use?

My Family of Dreamers

Malala Yousafzai

Walt Disney

Advay Ramesh

Shakira

William Kamkwamba

Roberto Clemente

Write your name: _____

15

MALALA YOUSAFZAI

Pakistan, 1997

"As our politicians are doing nothing for us, nothing for peace, nothing for education, I want to become prime minister of my country. To some people this seems too much – they feel you can't dream that way; you must have a smaller dream. But sometimes, it's good to dream bigger. This is what I've been telling our world leaders: dream big, make your ambitions bigger."

A lot of people were surprised when the Norwegian Nobel Committee presented the **Nobel Peace Prize** to Malala Yousafzai, a 17 year-old Pakistani woman who, in 2014, became the youngest person in history to receive this award.

What did Malala do to deserve the Nobel Peace Prize? There's little you can say in words about the heroic acts of many people who overcome fear to defend their rights and the rights of others. Malala's determination to defend women's rights in her country to receive an education almost cost her her life when a follower of the Taliban movement shot her in the head. At barely 11 years old, Malala manifested her passion for education and expressed her dream of becoming a doctor, which went against the subjugation of the Taliban. Unfortunately, there are places in the world where human rights are violated, and people like Malala have had to put their lives at risk to fight for them and create fairer societies.

I'm BRAVE

Nine months after the attack, Malala raised her voice at a United Nations meeting, with greater vigor than before. She expressed the urgency and importance of supporting her causes. Since her intervention at the United Nations, Malala has received the support of multiple organizations. She also created the "Malala Fund" to aid 60 million girls worldwide who do not go to school. Despite her traumatic experience, Malala has preferred to focus on the positive and do what she can to promote change.

Today, Malala lives in England with her parents and two siblings, and although she wishes to return to her home in Pakistan, she cannot do so. Hers and her family's lives are in danger. In an interview, Malala commented that she misses her friends and teachers and that, sometimes, her mind travels to her garden. "I planted flowers and seeds on it and, right in the middle, a mango tree. I would stand in the garden at night and look at the stars. Here in the UK, I've noticed you don't really see stars."

Malala acknowledges the inspiration she has received from her father, Ziauddin Yousafzai, a schoolteacher. He encouraged the passion for education in her daughter and supported her in this fight against injustice. "He is the one who taught me to stand up and fight. Change makes a difference, and one has to keep fighting and never give up."

At the opening of her movie "He Named Me Malala," our dreamer expressed her hopes that the film would help spread the message about the importance of children's right to education.

"We all can create change. I'm an ordinary girl, no different than any other girl, but I choose not to be silent. I choose to speak up and raise my voice for equality. All of us can use our voices to fight for equality and education."

Malala

17

MALALA'S TREASURE CHEST OF WORDS

peace
Politics
Inclusion Power
Quality Rights
Change Injustice
subjugate EDUCATION
Equity Equality
Fight Inspiration

#6 Read our dreamer's story and write the number of the Sustainable Development Goals addressed in each diamond.

#7 Help us complete the meaning of 3 words from Malala's treasure chest that are key in education:
1. **Inclusion is...**
2. **Equality is...**
3. **Quality is...**

THINKERS' TABLE **#8**

The power of education

Inspired by Malala and the children and adults who do not have access to education, we invite you to participate in a forum about the following topics:

- Why do you think there is still illiteracy in some parts of the world?
- What are the consequences of the lack of education in the personal and collective sphere?
- What is the current situation of girls in Pakistan?
- Are there other children in the world in this situation? How can we help?
- Why is it important for girls to receive an education?
- What happens when a child does not receive an education?
- How does this reflect in their family, in their city, in their country, and in the world?
- What was the education and teaching process like before the COVID-19 pandemic?
- How did it affect you? Why is physical interaction with your peers and teachers important?
- What do you think teaching and education will be like in the near future?
- **In a group, work on a document that brings together the most critical points of this forum and publish it in your school newspaper with your teacher's help.**

Your voice counts!

Select the word from Malala's treasure chest of words that corresponds to each meaning in the following list:

- _____: action and effect of change. Leaving one thing or situation to take on another.
- _____: the condition of being able to demand what is considered ethically correct. Example: human rights.
- _____: upbringing, teaching, and doctrine given to children and young people. Instruction through teaching action.
- _____: to fail rights, reason and equity. Absence of justice.
- _____: equivalence of two quantities or expressions. Identical treatment. Example: all human beings have the right to be recognized as equal before the law.
- _____: action and effect of inspiring or being inspired. The stimulus that animates the creative work in art or science.
- _____: action of two forces acting in the opposite direction. Fight, dispute.
- _____: the healthy coexistence between human beings, in which citizens have the same opportunities, and their fundamental rights are respected.
- _____: science and statecraft.
- _____: to subdue or dominate someone using fear and/or force.
- _____: power, strength, capacity, possibility, power, domain, command.

A garden full of stars for Malala ACTIVITY #10

- I invite you to be inspired by this story and draw in your workbook or large cardboard a garden for Malala as a sign of support for her cause.
- Propose to your teachers the idea of creating a garden in your school dedicated to those who fight and contribute to the education of the children of the world.
- Write a poem inspired by education.
- What do you want to study when you go to university? Write a letter to yourself where you talk about your goals and the importance of studying for the career you want.

¡M__ v__e c__unts!

WALT DISNEY

United States, 1901-1966

"If you can dream it, you can do it!"

Did you know that Walt Disney was an artist, director, screenwriter, producer, and cartoon series animator, who received an Oscar award 32 times? And that he is considered an icon in the history of children's animation cinema and a revolutionary in the world of entertainment?

One of the most magical sites in the universe is called Disneyland, and fortunately for us earthlings, we do not have to change planets to see it. We can turn on the TV and enjoy the whole family of cartoons that Walt Disney left us.

HOW DID HE DO IT?

The best way to know the answer is by getting to know his story!

Walter Elias Disney, «Walt», was born in Chicago to a humble family. His paternal grandparents were Irish immigrants living in Canada, where Flora and Elijah, his parents, were born. Walt spent his early years living on a farm with his family, where he developed a deep love for animals that inspired his early drawings. In 1911 the family moved to Kansas City, where his father bought a newspapers distribution route on which Walt and his brother Roy worked for six years. The day began at 4:30 in the morning before going to school. It continued into the evening with a run for one of the newspapers. The schedule was strenuous and impacted his school performance.

To improve his skills, he took some advanced courses and specialized in art and photography. He tried to enlist in the military service, but they did not accept him because he was very young. He decided to serve in the Red Cross instead and was sent to France to work as an ambulance driver. True to his passion, he decorated the ambulances he drove with his drawings. After this experience, he returned to the United States. And even though he had several jobs in the artistic field, he faced a period of job instability and serious economic difficulties before achieving success.

Walt was not satisfied with just creating exceptional drawings. He wanted to take his creations to a higher level: animation. Walt knew that to get to where he wanted to be, he needed to give everything he had. And so, he spared no hours or resources in producing sketches, creating characters, and writing scripts, for he was also an excellent storyteller.

Despite being a master at what he did, he knew how to listen and was receptive to constructive criticism and the ideas of others. His innovations include the first cartoons with synchronized sound and the first animated feature film.

In 1922, at the age of 21, he managed to raise funds from several neighbors and friends and founded Laugh-O-Gram Studio. Still, he filed for bankruptcy soon after despite having produced two successful short films. The only thing he could save from the economic disaster was his camera and a copy of his most original work: "Alice in Wonderland." They say that at this point in his life, marked by hunger and misery, Walt Disney found the inspiration to create his most famous character: Mickey Mouse.

Small jobs in advertising served Walt to slowly recover from his economic situation until he decided to leave Kansas City and move to Hollywood. Not able to find employment in a city that already was a mecca of cinema, Walt, joined by his brother Roy O. Disney, founded the Disney Brothers Cartoon Studio. In it, they filmed the short Alice Comedies and got a contract for a twelve-episode series with a distributor of animated drawings. Excited about this triumph, he hired the best professionals in the industry and started the production of the animated series *Alice in Wonderland*. After this project, they successfully produced the *Oswald the Rabbit cartoon series*. *Nevertheless*, Walt is unable to reach a fair compensation agreement with Universal Pictures, which was the distributor for the project, and decides not to continue with his contract. Unfortunately, Walt Disney had allowed Universal Pictures to register the *Oswald Rabbit cartoon series* rights and, therefore, lost his work. A mistake he never made again.

Walt faced another economic crisis. He was left without a work team, except for Ubee Iwerks, who stayed with him. Together they gave life to Mortimer Mouse, the universal icon that, thanks to his wife, Lillian Disney, was renamed as Mickey Mouse. However, it would be long before Mickey Mouse achieved the popularity and recognition he deserved. Years later, Walt Disney triumphs with *Snow White and the Seven Dwarves* and becomes a millionaire. This film was followed by other animated creations, including *Pinocchio*, *Fantasia*, *Dumbo*, and *Bambi*.

But Walt Disney, believing that **«all dreams are possible if we have the courage to pursue them,»** did not feel satisfied by only giving us his magical audiovisual world. He wanted to go beyond the screen. Make us live the magic so that everyone could feel it and enjoy it as an authentic experience. This dream was called Disneyland, and although Walt had difficulty finding investors who believed in the feasibility of the project, he did not give up until he achieved it. That is how on October 5th, 1955, the magical world of Disney opened its doors to the public in Anaheim, California, providing entertainment, happiness, and hundreds of thousands of jobs in its multiple business initiatives.

From that day on, the world of entertainment changed forever, and planet Earth was dressed in magic!

Walt Disney is a legend of the twentieth century. He carved out his triumph with effort, passion, and vision.

WALT DISNEY'S

#11 Read our dreamer's story and write the number of the Sustainable Development Goals addressed in each diamond.

Creativity

Entertainment

Scourge

Caricature

Icon

Distributor

Imagination

Investor

Passion

Screenplay   sketch

Film

Economic crisis

Character

Vision

ACTIVITIES

#12 What learning experiences can you take from this story?

- _____: Basic and simple trial or scheme, without much detail, before executing a project.
- _____: Exaggerated graphic figure or portrait in which the features and the appearance of a person or thing are deformed.
- _____: Faculty or ability to do or create a thing with originality. The disposition that drives individuals to invent, discover and create.
- _____: Person or entity that markets or distributes products; is the intermediary between the producer and the buyer.
- _____: What serves as fun, recreation, or hobby.
- _____: A writing containing the dialogues for a motion picture film, play, or tv show.
- _____: A sign that identifies an idea or an object. A person or thing which is representative of an ideology or historical moment.
- _____: People or companies that have money or capital and use it to make some profit.
- _____: People's ability to invent, create, find solutions; action and effect of mentally imagining or forming images.
- _____: Intense feeling towards another person, oneself, some activity, sport, or idea.
- _____: A work of cinematographic art in which a true story or fiction is narrated in an audiovisual way.
- _____: Important or prominent person. In a play, it can be human beings, animals, or objects involved in the action.
- _____: Action and effect of seeing. Comprehension capacity, particularly when it is correct.
- _____: Onslaught, catastrophe, negative fact that affects deeply. A calamity or misfortune.
- _____: It is characterized by a decrease in employment, consumption, and investment, which can reach a more severe state called recession.

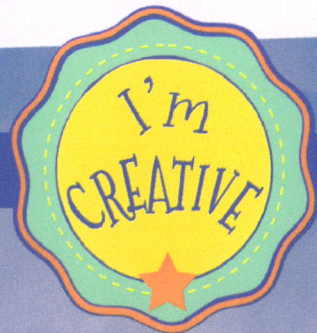

I'm CREATIVE

ACTIVITIES #14

- Discover three similar nouns with different meanings: **emigrant, migrant, and immigrant.** What do these words mean?

STEP 1. Research various sources and analyze the information from different points of view.

STEP 2. Write in your workbook the results of your research and what you think about it.

STEP 3. Organize a conversation with your classmates and your family about the questions presented at each thinkers' table.

The story of our dreamer Walt Disney is like a key that opens a rich thematic treasure chest, ideal for research and reflection. Remember that every human being can be part of the solution. What you think, feel and dream with determination can turn into action if you gather the courage and take the first step.

THINKERS' TABLE

#15 Investigate what the UN agency UNHCR does for refugees.

- Disney's parents came from immigrant families. What are the causes and consequences of immigration?
- Imagine you had to go to another country without taking anything with you, and where the language and customs are different. How do you think you would feel?
- What would your needs be? How would you like people to receive you and help you?
- Where are mass exoduses of the population occurring globally, and what is triggering them?
- How can this unfortunate situation be solved? What will happen if it is not resolved?
- What is the impact of the 2030 Agenda on this problem?

The United Nations (UN) indicates that by the end of 2018, nearly 71 million people in the world were forced to leave their homes due to conflicts and persecution. Of these 70 million, 30 million are refugees, and half of those are young people under 18.

During his childhood and due to this family's poverty, Walt Disney and his brother had to work as if they were adults. Aware of this situation, Disney's conglomerate companies implemented a code of conduct that prohibits child labor and exploitation for all manufacturers of the products they consume. Other companies have done the same. However, millions of children must work to survive in today's world.

Investigate and discuss in a group the following questions:

- In which countries is child labor used?
- What are the reasons generating this phenomenon?
- Which are the industries that employ children, and how do they benefit?
- Think about the children who have to work. What are the consequences, and how do you think they feel?
- Think about the child, the region, and the country where this happens. How will their future be? Do you consider that these cases are isolated and do not affect you?
- Are there any international laws to protect children? Are those who violate such laws sanctioned?

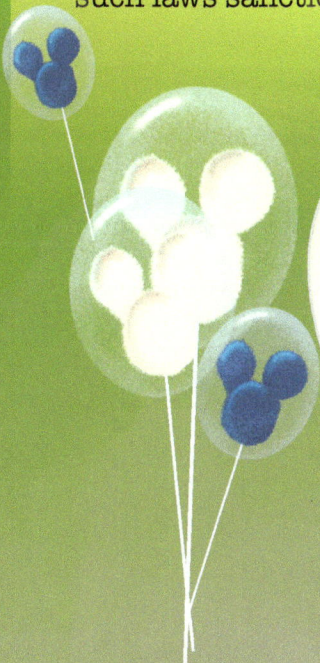

#17

Based on this research, select a case that has called your attention. It could be a community, country or something that happens in an industry. Present your arguments about what should be done so the affected children do not have to work and can enjoy a safe and healthy childhood with opportunities for their future. Select at least two of the 17 Sustainable Development Goals that would contribute to your solution.

BE CREATIVE!

Did you know that, according to UNICEF, approximately one in ten children in the world (152 million) works, and half of them do so in dangerous conditions?

#18 In the story about Walt Disney, you can find several words that define his personality or important aspects of his life.
Can you find these words or phrases?

Which Disney character do you like best and why?

How do you imagine your childhood would have been without Walt Disney's characters?

#19 Look in Walt Disney's treasure chest of words to find four magic words that will help you reach your goals!

C

P

V

I

Add your own magic keys!

"Creativity is contagious, pass it on."
Albert Einstein

Time to be creative

#20

I would love to meet your pet. If you have one, please introduce us. Cut an image and paste it in the following spaces if you do not have one.
You can also draw it!

Draw your pet (if you do not have one, draw the pet you wish to have)

#21 Let's draw with **words!**

Hello, Sakura. The name of the pet I send you is_____ and belongs to the family of_____. It is a very _____ animal species and lives in_____. I know you have never seen a _____ in your life and that you will __ this pet. I hope you like it as much I do! Its body is _____

, it has _____. Its skin is _____

_____ it seems _____ when you touch it. It eats _____

_____. It has_____ and its_____ looks like _____

_____

_____. When it gets upset, it sounds like this: _____ similar to _____

_____. I advise you to __

_____

_____. It needs _____

_____

_____ to survive. You can teach it to

_____

_____. It likes _____

_____. If you want to keep it in a special place, you can choose between _____ or

_____. I think your pet will feel very _____ there.

DO NOT FORGET TO SEND ME YOUR DRAWING.
I ALSO WANT TO COLLECT NEW PETS.

Sincerely,

Your Name _____.

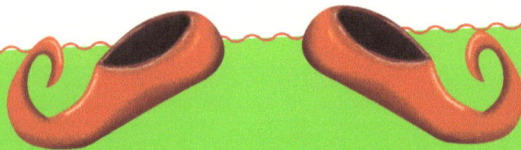

"Every child is an artist, the problem
is how to remain an artist when he grows up".

Pablo Picasso

CREATING IS FUN

Draw that pet now!

You already have your first caricature.
Just like Walt Disney once did!

LISTEN TO THE VOICE OF SHAKIRA

Colombia, 1977

"In this life, to earn your place in the world, you must fight for it."

PERFORMER, SONGWRITER, PHILANTHROPIST, AND UNICEF GOODWILL AMBASSADOR.

You will surely be surprised to learn about the history of one of the most famous artists of the century: Shakira, whose name means *grateful and full of grace.*

Experts say that every minute two hundred babies are born in the world. A girl was born on one of those minutes of February 2, 1977, in Barranquilla, Colombia. Her parents baptized her as Shakira Isabel Mebarak Ripoll.

Her childhood transpired in a multicultural environment influenced by her Spanish and Arab roots. She expressed her love of singing and dancing from an early age. By the age of four, she had already written her first poem. At eight, she dedicated her first song titled "Your Dark Glasses" to her father. While other girls her age played with dolls or friends, she practiced and trained to be a professional singer.

Although her parents recognized her talent, her debut in the entertainment world was not easy. In an interview given by Shakira to the French magazine Closer, she commented that her music teacher did not want her to be part of the choir «... she thought that my voice was inharmonic, and my vibrato too pronounced. Some of the students, who are still good friends of mine, kept telling me I sang like a goat. I remember many days coming home sad, and my father told me not to change my vibrato, that one day **Shakira's** voice would play on all the radios"[1].

Her parents took her to different radio and television shows. Her Lebanese grandmother taught her Belly Dancing so she would not lose her traditions. At the age of ten, Shakira was an expert dancer, singing and writing songs. She achieved her first triumphs in artistic competitions at eleven. And at fourteen, she signed her first contract with Sony Music Colombia for an album with songs of her own authorship. Despite this achievement, Shakira experienced rejection when her voice was not appreciated, and her early albums were not as successful. The same happened when she dabbed into the acting world, in which she was criticized for her physical appearance. However, Shakira did not give up her dream. She continued to work on perfecting her talents, overcoming constant criticism until she achieved what many artists could not: becoming a «pioneer who has redefined the reach of Latin American singers and has become one of the most fascinating voices of today's Latin Pop/Rock music.»[2]

In 2017, the singer announced to the world that she was suffering from bleeding in her vocal cords, a disease that prevented her from singing. «Those were the hardest months of my life. Many times I wondered why I was going through so many obstacles. There were days when I didn't feel like getting up. I never thought I could lose my voice. I thought I'd lose a lot of other things in life, but never my voice. When I found myself in that situation, those were the hardest days," she confessed. Fortunately, Shakira has returned to singing.

Who does not remember songs like "Ojos Así" ("Eyes Like These"), "Pies Descalzos" ("Barefeet"), or "Ciega, Sorda, Muda" ("Blind, Deaf, Mute")? With them, Shakira conquered millions of fans and consolidated herself as one of the world's most beloved artists. Her success has allowed her to make another dream come true: helping in different social causes, including education for the most vulnerable. In 1997 she created the Pies Descalzos Foundation, which provides education, health, nutrition, and psychological assistance services to thousands of children in Colombia, Haiti, and South Africa through institutional partnerships. Another organization founded by Shakira is Latin America in Solidarity Action (ALAS, for its acronym in Spanish) to promote early childhood development in Latin America. Shakira was appointed UNICEF Goodwill Ambassador in 2003 for her dedication to children's well-being and future. She also received the Spirit of Hope Award in 2006 for her humanitarian work. More than 10,000 children and 67,000 young people and adults have benefited from her commitment to education.

Shakira has built a family with soccer player Gerard Piqué. They are the happy parents of Milan and Sacha. In addition to being one of the most awarded women in music, she is considered the most influential artist of her generation for her universal impact. Forbes magazine listed her as one of the 100 Most Influential Women on the Planet in 2015. In 2016, she received the World Economic Forum Crystal Award for her support of education and children. In her speech, the artist pointed out that investing in education generates miracles:

«Throughout my life, I have seen education work miracles; I have seen lives and even entire communities transform. And believe me, seeing a child who had no chance of success manages to move forward and get equal opportunities in adulthood is such a satisfying feeling that it even surpasses that of winning a Grammy».

Shakira

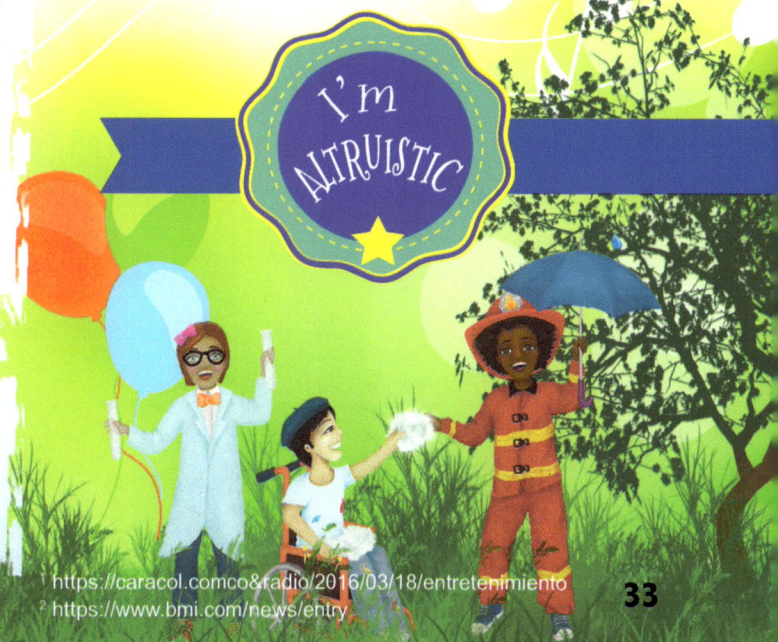

I'm ALTRUISTIC

SHAKIRA'S TREASURE CHEST OF WORDS

success
Artist
Entertainment
Determination
Social Causes
Discipline
Ambassador   Composer
innovator   PHILANTHROPY
Multicultural   Perfectionist
Poem   Vulnerable

#23 Read our dreamer's story and write the number of the Sustainable Development Goals addressed in each diamond.

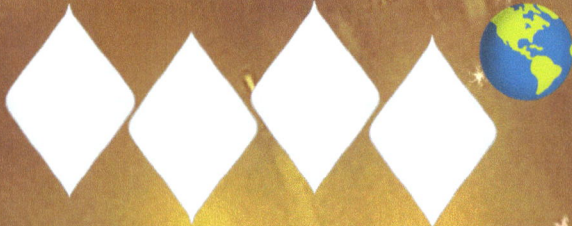

ACTIVITIES

#24

Select the word from Shakira's treasure chest of words that corresponds to each meaning in the following list:

- _____: a person who practices or cultivates any of the fine arts.
- The _____ were six: architecture, sculpture, painting, music, declamation and dance. Declamation includes poetry and music includes theater. This is why cinema is often called today the seventh art.
- _____: set of rules or norms whose compliance leads to a certain result.
- _____: action and effect of taking a resolution, of setting something specific to achieve an effect or whatever you want.
- _____: refers to problems affecting the development or progress of a sector of the population, for example, poverty, malnutrition, lack of education, and pollution, among others.
- _____: person who composes or writes a literary work or piece of music.
- _____: person who carries a message and is recognized as the highest representative of an entity or country.
- _____: love of mankind. Help offered to humanity without expecting anything in return.
- _____: person who reforms or changes something, adding new features. Someone who sets new standards.
- _____: allusive to various cultures and diversity in a society.
- _____: person who tends to improve something indefinitely. Person looking for perfection in what he/she does.
- _____: literary composition written in verses, where the author (the poet) expresses his emotions using rhyme and literary figures.
- _____: the quality someone has of being injured, damaged or harmed.
- _____: is the effect or the right consequence of an action or an undertaking. A happy or positive result of what you want to achieve.

ACTIVITIES

THINKERS' TABLE

#25

Write a poem inspired by what you have learned or what impressed you the most about Shakira's story.

#26

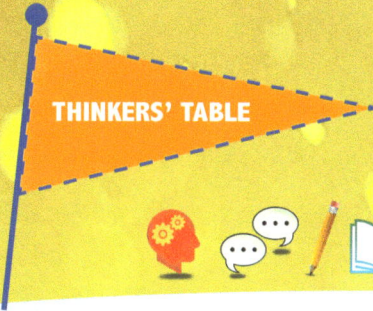

- Pick 5 people and ask them to answer the following questions. Write the answers on your workbook and share them with your thinkers' table.

PERSON	DO YOU FEEL LIKE A SUCCESSFUL PERSON? WHY?	WHAT HAVE BEEN YOUR GREATEST LIFE ACCOMPLISHMENTS?	WERE YOU CRITICIZED? DID YOU HAVE SUPPORT? DID ANYONE MOTIVATE YOU? DID ANYONE HELP YOU?	WHICH OBSTACLES DID YOU HAVE TO OVERCOME TO BE SUCCESSFUL OR TO ACHIEVE YOUR MOST DESIRED GOAL?
#1				
#2				
#3				
#4				
#5				

a

At the Thinkers' Table, define the meaning of success and what is needed to achieve it.

b

Learn about Teresa of Calcula and reflect on her quote: "I can do things you cannot, you can do things I cannot; together we can do great things."

35

#27

Talk about the following questions:

a

Do you think we can end world poverty if we all unite toward that goal?

b

Can you contribute in a more effective way to solve the problems of others when you are successful?

c

How do you feel about people living in poverty or children unable to go to school? How does their situation affects yours?

d

How can you be part of the solution?

#28

Activity: Experiment with the communion between music and your body.

- Select a piece of music with no words (lyrics) and close your eyes. Let yourself be carried away by the music and allow your body to express itself with free movements.

- Repeat this exercise with other musical pieces, some traditional to your country and from other countries. Listen to the rhythm of the drums, flutes, piano, guitars, harps, maracas, trombones, harmonicas, or clapping of hands, and do not think about the aesthetics or perfection of the movements. Just experiment with the language of music in your body.

#29

Group activity

Musical event. Students, teachers, parents, and community members can participate in this activity. The aim is to join forces, talents, and ideas in stimulating the spirit of solidarity for those in need. Working together, the students will organize an artistic event to raise funds for a local organization to aid children living in shelters.

• With their teachers' help, a team will be appointed to support the project's logistics. This team must select the organization that will receive the aid. The team must choose the different acts included in the event, for example, a play that includes singing and dancing, a musical event, or a poetry recital.

• According to the talents and interests of the students, organize groups to assign the following tasks, as defined by the type of event:

  • Writing the script of the play
  • Composition of the lyrics for a song
  • Music
  • Choreography and costumes
  • Ticket sales or donations collection
  • Publicity for the event
  • Organizing the presentation
  • Performance for the children, if possible, and presentation of donations.

Let me tell you a story...

When fishermen lacking proper navigation systems enter the sea, it's almost, it is impossible for them to know whether they are violating territorial laws or another country's maritime border, as borders at sea are invisible. The problem is most critical when there are disputes between nations.

In Tamil Nadu, southern India, fishermen who cross the invisible maritime borders of their neighboring country, the island nation of Sri Lanka, are detained for months and punished with fines that sometimes are impossible to pay. For centuries, these two countries lived in harmony. They exchanged migratory flow, shared bonds of ethnicity, language, religion, and the waters of Palk Bay. This is the strait that separates the state of Tamil Nadu in India and the Jaffna district of Sri Lanka's northernmost province, which is a rich fishing area. Fishing is part of the economy and history of this region.

The fishermen's situation worried Advay Ramesh, a 14-year-old teenager and undergraduate student at the National Public School of Chennai (Madras), the capital of Tamil Nadu state. The empathy and concern he felt for them and their families inspired him to develop an easy-to-use mobile global positioning system (GPS) that allows fishermen to identify their routes using an app built around a satellite navigation system. This new little device, which Advay called FELT (FishErmen Lifeline Terminal), warns fishermen when they are nearing the maritime border.

At first, Advay thought only about developing an app. But fortunately, he went further and created a mobile device that uses an open Standard Position Services (SPS) system from India's Regional Satellite Navigation System.

38

His invention was the winner in Asia of the Google Community Impact Award 2016 at the Google Science Fair, which rewards innovative and creative proposals to improve people's lives. Thousands of science and engineering students from more than 107 countries participated in this competition, where award-winning youth receive student scholarships and funds to perfect their creations.

His invention not only pinpoints maritime borders but also allows fishermen to keep a daily record of their route. It also marks and stores those points where fishing was good, so they can return and notify them if they are sailing towards a storm.

It is estimated that at least fifteen million people work in India's fishing industry. Can you imagine the repercussions of this invention for the fishing community in Tamil Nadu, India, and around the world? Can you imagine how Advay's life changed while making his invention and when his project won the competition?

Advay Ramesh's story has gone around the world and inspired children and adults. He certainly has a dream and a vision of what he wants for his life and the life of many other people.

In one of the many interviews Advay gave, he commented on the situation of the fishermen, stating: **"It takes too long for them to be released, and I wanted to help this community."**

India

Sri Lanka

THINKERS' TABLE

#30

- Organize several groups of thinkers and formulate at least three solutions that may contribute to renewing harmony between these two nations and improving the quality of life of the fishermen and their families.
- Present the solutions and provide references to support them.

When Advay was asked about his future plans, he replied: **"I would like to go to the United States to study engineering after I graduate."**

And now I ask you: what are your plans for the future?

#31 Read our dreamer's story and write the number of the Sustainable Development Goals addressed in each diamond.

Dispute
Critical
Community
AFFLICTION
Inspire
Borders   Empathy
Harmony

ACTIVITY **#32**

Select the word from Advay Ramesh's treasure chest of words that corresponds to each meaning in the following list:

- _____: are delimitations, separations. They can be real or imaginary lines that demarcate territories.
- _____: a state of peace, balance and understanding.
- _____: feeling or ability to identify with the other, their feelings, reality, or situation.
- _____: to awaken a feeling, some ideas, or provoke the desire to do something that favors creativity, ingenuity, and action.
- _____: a feeling of annoyance, sadness, anguish, worry, sorrow, and restlessness.
- _____: group of people who, in addition to sharing the same geographical location, they present common elements that unite them, such as language, values, customs, interests, among others.
- _____: refers to a difficult situation or time of risk and severity.
- _____: situation where differences occur generating a conflict or strife, a struggle.

ACTIVITIES

a

Research
the meaning of the following terms and, as much as you can, write it in your own words:
- Maritime borders
- Migration flow

b

Research
about the ethnicities of your country. Select the one that calls your attention and write at least three aspects that identify them.

c

Research
how a mobile positioning system work and draw it on your workbook. Think about the uses you could give it to benefit your community.

d

Think
about a problem in your community and about an invention that would help you solve it. Let your imagination and creativity run wild. Draw your invention on your workbook and write: What is it? What is it for? How does it work?

ACTIVITY #34

Build the map of your dreams

Today is a great day! We will make all the dreams that live in our minds and hearts come true. We will prove that they are as real as everything we perceive with our senses.

STEP 1

Close your eyes and put both hands on your heart. Feel it beating.

STEP 2

Keep your eyes closed and your hands over your heart. Concentrate on your dreams. Let your mind and your spirit communicate. Feel how your heartbeat goes faster when you think about your dreams. It is exciting!

STEP 3

Now we are ready!
For this activity, you must use materials that inspire you and that are your favorite:

- Magazines
- Christmas or Birthday cards
- Photos
- Glitter
- Letters of the alphabet

- Stickers
- Scissors
- Glue
- Tape
- Poster board or cardboard

STEP 4

- Using a pencil, divide the poster board into four parts.
- On the top part, write: My map of dreams.
- In each quadrant, write the titles: Do, Go, Be, and Love.

STEP 5

Now say out loud the magic words:
Let my vision open up with all the dreams of my heart!

HISABOOM !

STEP 6

Answer the following questions and illustrate the responses in each quadrant that you drew on the poster board. Use your imagination and express yourself through drawings, words, or magazine clippings. **Each letter of the magic word will help you decipher your dream map.**

Go
1. Which places would you like to visit?
2. What would you like to do there?
3. Who would you go with?
4. How would you get there?

Love
1. Who do you love?
2. What do you love?
3. What makes you feel loved?
4. How, or in what way, do you show that love?

Do
1. What would you like to do as an adult?
2. What sort of person would you like to be? Remember that there are people that are kind, helpful, happy, humanitarian... and that we are much more than a job.
3. What do you want to do during your next vacation?
4. What would you like to learn?

Be
1. If you could help someone, who would you help?
2. How would you help?
3. What can you do to be a better human being?
4. What do you want to be?

Boom!!!
1. What is important for you?
2. What activities do you like the most?
3. Of all those activities, which one would you like to do forever?
4. What cannot be missing in your life?
5. What do you need to do to make sure you have what you consider important in your life?

STEP 7

WRITE THE DATE, AND DON'T FORGET TO WRITE YOUR NAME ON THE MAP OF DREAMS.

STEP 8

Hang your map of dreams in a place where you can see it every day, and remember that your dreams are the path to your happiness. **YOUR DREAMS ARE WAITING FOR YOU!**

I'M EMPATHIC

WILLIAM KAMKWAMBA

Malawi, 1997

"I looked at my father and looked at those dry fields; it was a future I could not accept."

It was the year 2001, and Malawi, one of the poorest countries in Africa, was suffering a catastrophic famine. Climate conditions and the decrease of cultivating lands had affected the maize reserves in three neighboring countries: Malawi, Zambia, and Zimbabwe. Prices went up due to food scarcity, and millions of people faced hunger and many other shortages.

The picture in Malawi was bleak. The number of victims increased by hundreds of thousands, and drought and floods gave no respite.

Maize imports did not arrive on time or in the quantities that were needed. Famine threatened at least four million people in the south of the African continent.

At the home of William Kamkwamba, a fourteen-year-old teenager, there was also hunger and anguish. That year, his parents were not able to pay his tuition for high school. The few resources they had only allowed them to eat once a day: at night. That is how he and his seven sisters survived.

William Kamkwamba felt very sad. His hopes of studying and improving his quality of life seemed to have evaporated for reasons outside his control. However, while others lamented their misfortune, he gathered his courage and set out to find a solution.

"Before I discovered the wonders of science, I was just a simple farmer in a country of poor farmers. But one year, our fortune turned very bad..."

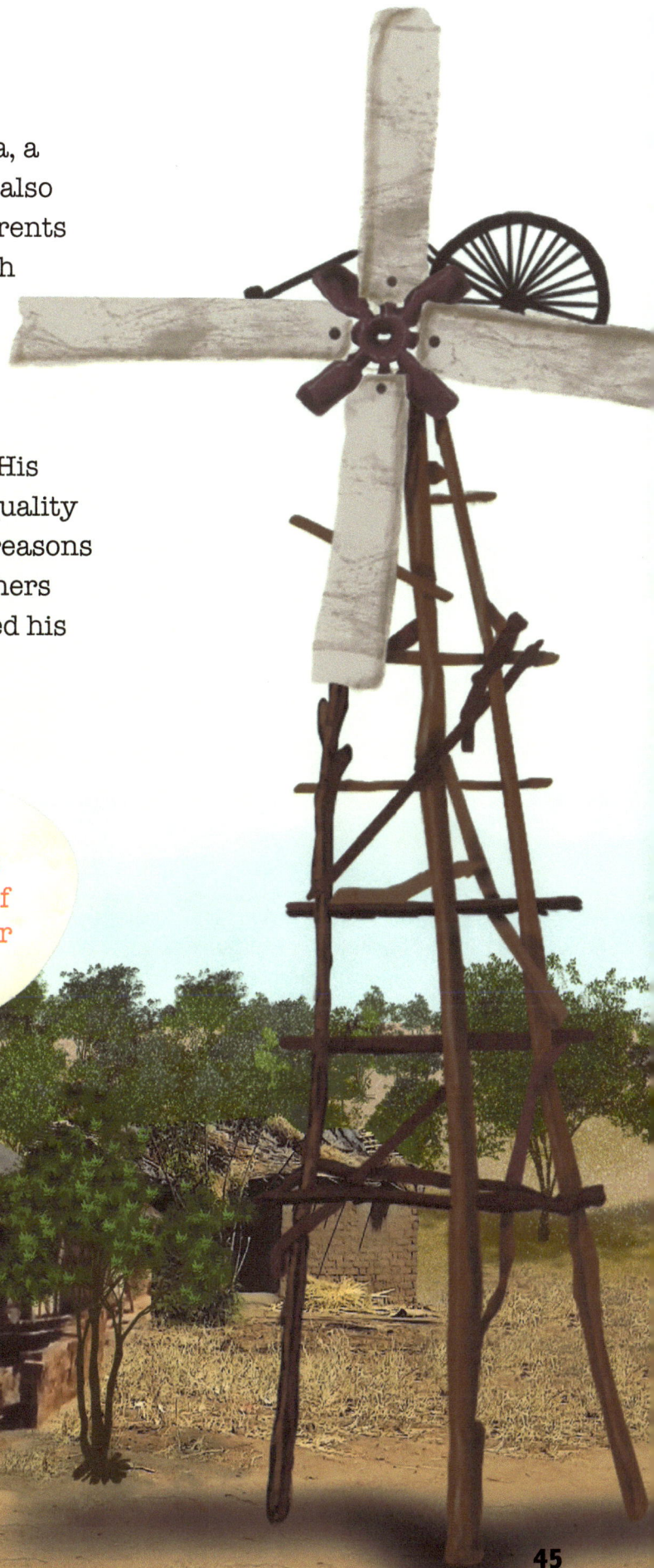

And what better ally than books?

He thought...

Without delay, he took refuge in the library, and even though the books were written in English, he did not give up. He strove to understand the graphs and did not stop. Until, one day, the answer he was searching for appeared in a book titled *Using Energy*: it was a beautiful **windmill.**

The windmill could **generate electricity** and pump water, which meant irrigation, a defense against the famine they were facing. Now William Kamkwamba faced the next challenge, obtaining the materials to build it.

And how do you think he built it? Well, with ingenuity, self-confidence, and persistence. He did not mind the criticism or the discouraging comments. He walked, knocked on doors, and went out in search of junk. And that is how, with the blade from a fan, a shock absorber, the remains of a bicycle, tree trunks, and pieces of PVC pipe, he put together his first mill. And, best of all, he brought electricity to his home.

Twelve watts of power were enough to turn on four light bulbs and two radios. Can you imagine the surprise on the faces of his family and neighbors? William Kamkwamba wanted the fifty houses in his village, called Masitala, to benefit from his invention since they lacked electricity and drinking water. To do this, he had to build a windmill of greater capacity and install a water pump and a drip irrigation system.

The news spread like wildfire. It crossed continents, and while he was working on getting the resources to build more mills, people from the science world were looking for him. That is how in 2007 and at the age of 19, and after several weeks of intense search, people from the TED program found him and invited him to come forward and talk about his experience. William Kamkwamba became famous and got investors to contribute the capital he needed for his projects.

"Before that time, I had never been away from my home. I had not seen a computer. I had never gone on the Internet and had never seen an airplane."

William Kamkwamba is considered a hero by his people. He was able to finish high school, get into college, and start a promising career in science and entrepreneurship as an inventor. He has been invited for visitsby multiple organizations, including Google, and has received many accolades.

He wrote his autobiography, *The Boy Who Harnessed the Wind*, which has sold more than a million copies. It has been translated to at least twenty languages and brought to the screen by Netflix. The child of the windmills became a renowned inventor who went ahead with his project and inspired the world to challenge poverty and build a better future.

"To invent something, all you need is imagination and a big pile of junk."

Thomas Alva Edison

Learn more about our dreamer's life on his web page: http://www.williamkamkwamba.com/

WILLIAM KAMKWAMBA'S ACTIVITY

#35 Read our dreamer's story and write the number of the Sustainable Development Goals addressed in each diamond.

Autobiography
Inventor
Imports
Electricity
Energy
Scarcity
Climate change
Famine
Reserves

#36

Select the word from William Kamkwamba's treasure chest of words that corresponds to each meaning in the following list:

- _____: widespread and prolonged shortages of basic foodstuffs.

- _____: save to something, as a precaution, to serve in a determined moment. Countries hold reserves of resources, which can be in gold and currency rates. There are also oil and food reserves.

- _____: lack of essential resources to meet needs and livelihoods, including water, food, energy, housing, medicines, etc.

- _____: global variation of the Earth's climate.

- _____: goods or services brought from another country. Countries export or sell and import or purchase goods and services. This type of marketing is an exchange that favors distribution and production, among other factors.

- _____: ability of bodies to perform work and produce changes in themselves or in other bodies. It's the ability to make things work.

- _____: is a form of energy, a physical phenomenon caused by electrical charges at rest or movement.

- _____: refers to the person who has invented or created something or is engaged in inventing.

- _____: is an account of the episodes of a person's life.

ACTIVITY

DID YOU KNOW THAT STATISTICS CHANGE EVERY DAY AND THAT MANY OF THESE FIGURES DEPEND ON ACTIONS AND DECISIONS WE MAKE INDIVIDUALLY OR COLLECTIVELY?

Year 2021

The world's population is 7.9 billion people.
Today, enough food is produced to feed 10 billion.
Should we produce less food?

Of the approximately 7.9 billion people,
821 million are 'chronically malnourished.'
What actions would help reduce these numbers?

The projections show that if this trend continues, hunger will
exceed 840 million people by 2030.
**How can we change this projection to end hunger
in the year 2030?**

YEAR 2030

I'm CLEVER

THINKERS' TABLE

#38

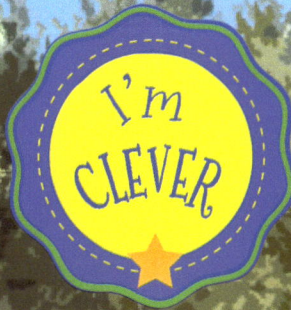

"The formulation of a problem is often more essential than its solution."

Albert Einstein

STEP 1

GATHER A GROUP OF THINKERS AND BRAINSTORM BASED ON THE FOLLOWING QUESTIONS:

1 According to reports from the United Nations, the world produces enough food for all humanity. So why is hunger on the rise in some parts of the world?

2 According to various reports, humanity wastes between 30% and 40% of the food produced.
- Why does food waste happen?
- Do you think some countries waste more than others?
- Can anything be done to reduce waste?

3 Many people believe that climate change is not real. Inquire about this topic and answer the following questions:
- What is climate change? Why do you think some people and organizations claim it is a lie or fallacy?
- How can climate affect people's lives and the planet?
- What measures should governments take to ensure that there is food for all inhabitants of the planet?
- If no action is taken now, what will happen to the life of the different species on Earth?

SELECT 3 POINTS THAT YOU CONSIDER MOST RELEVANT FROM THIS THINKERS' TABLE AND ELABORATE STRONG ARGUMENTS TO SUPPORT THEM IN A GROUP DISCUSSION.

STEP 3 NOW THAT YOU KNOW THE IMPORTANCE OF STOPPING FAMINE AND READY OURSELVES FOR WHAT MAY COME, WORK WITH YOUR GROUP ON 3 POSSIBLE SOLUTIONS THE WORLD COULD IMPLEMENT TO MEET THE ZERO HUNGER GOAL BY 2030. WHAT CAN YOU DO TO ACHIEVE THIS GOAL?

- Inspired by the story of our dreamer William Kamkwamba, search for information on **World Food Day** and the role of the Food and Agriculture Organization (FAO).
- Research in your area if some organizations or groups work to eradicate hunger from the planet and support them.
- Invite others to collaborate.

Alliances and collaborations are powerful!

Maize, the third cereal source of food in the world, and much more!

- It is believed that corn was first cultivated approximately 10 thousand years ago.
- More than 60 varieties of maize are part of our daily diet.
- It is a food staple in some countries.
- Maize and its by-products (syrup, oil, flour, or starch) are used to produce thousands of other products.
- **Did you know that corn is used to produce a fuel called bioethanol that replaces the gasoline used by cars?**

ACTIVITIES #39

There are many myths and legends about maize. In *Letter to My Dreams™ for the Children of the World*, we present three. Write a summary of the tale you have enjoyed the most and represent it through a drawing, just as you imagine it.

- We are going to **Mexico,** in **Central America**. Learn about the myth or traditional tale that tells the story about a supernatural being, the Aztec god Quetzalcoatl and the story of the arrival of maize.

- Let's continue to **Guatemala**. Let's delve into the Mayan civilization and its sacred book, the Popol Vuh. Legend has it that men first were made out of mud, then wood, and finally white and yellow corn...

- Now, let's travel to **Bolivia** in **South America**. Search for "The Legend of Corn." It says that in the region of Kollana, there were two communities formed by the ayllu Chayanta and the ayllu Charca, who lived in confrontation...

Discover the power of creativity

Fire, the wheel, the plow, gunpowder, concrete, the light bulb, the steam engine, the windmill, the printing press, the airplane, antibiotics, the telegraph, the combustion engine, the computer, the telephone, and the internet are some of the most valuable inventions of humanity.

The Persians of the fourth-century A.D. already used windmills for irrigation and grinding grain. However, our guest dreamer William Kamkwamba only knew about the existence of mills in the XXI century, which allowed him to bring electric light to his community. The same one that Thomas Alva Edison had invented in 1879, using a charred bamboo filament to make the first incandescent lamp stay on for more than 48 hours.

ACTIVITIES #40

Develop a project to create **a community orchard** in your school or neighborhood. Then gather the most important data and display it on a poster board or computer application. For this project, we need to:

1 Research how to make an orchard and understand the phases of the project with clarity.

2 Look for an appropriate place and analyze the advantages it offers.

3 Identify all the benefits of this project and its impact on the community.

4 Make a list of what is needed, for example, tools, soil, seeds, money, volunteers, etc.

5 Get ready and present your project to your parents, teachers, and friends to get their support. Together you can create this community orchard.

ROBERTO CLEMENTE

Puerto Rico, 1934-1972

"Any time you have an opportunity to make a difference in this world, and you don't, then you are wasting your time on Earth."

Hooome ruuun!

It was the year 1934, and the world was still facing the effects of the economic depression of 1929, the most severe in history, marked by extreme poverty and unemployment. At the time, San Antón, a neighborhood in the town of Carolina on the island of Puerto Rico was a community with less than fifteen hundred residents. Many families earned their livelihood in the sugar industry, including Melchor Clemente, a foreman in a sugar mill, and Luisa Walker, the parents of Roberto Clemente. The community's hardships and economic difficulties were somewhat dissipated by spending time with family and neighbors, listening to the radio, and following baseball, "the sport of the hot ball" games broadcasts.

Clemente was a stocky boy; he had a solid, athletic, agile, and vigorous body. His arms and legs were powerful, and his hands were said to be huge. They say that his first bat was a broomstick with which he hit balls made out of sauce cans and soda caps. He also played with handmade balls made out of stockings lined with tape. Roberto was not more than nine years old when he participated in his first baseball tournament sponsored by the Carolina Police Athletic League. There, he showcased his evident talent. That first event stirred in him what later would become a true passion for sports. As he grew older, he stood out as a softball and baseball player, a track and field athlete, and a javelin thrower.

Clemente grew up in a family with strong moral values and principles. His parents, teachers, and the Christian Church he attended had a profound impact on him. They were responsible for the values of respect, discipline, ethics, hard work, equality, transcendence of love, and service to others that characterized his actions throughout his life. He always found a way to help, from organizing volunteer work to cleaning the yard to raising money to build a fence for his school and rescuing a driver from a burning vehicle aand did all this, just as a child.

Aware of his potential, teachers and others who knew Roberto supported him in achieving his dream of becoming a professional baseball player.

A goal he gave preference to when he was offered scholarships from two universities.

Clemente devoted himself to baseball and reached the sport's top ranks with a lot of effort. People said he ran like a gazelle and that when he hit the ball, he had the strength of a thousand cannons. In 1952, at the age of 18, he went from Class A Baseball to Class AA, playing for the Juncos team, champions of the Puerto Rico Baseball League. Months later, he signed a contract as a professional winter baseball player with the Santurce Crabbers and became a big star in his homeland.

Although he had the ability and dreamed of representing Puerto Rico as part of their national team, he was never chosen for the selection.

"Everyone knows I've been a fighter all my life. I believe that every human being is equal, but one has to fight hard all the time to maintain that equality."

"I don't believe in color; I believe in people."

This experience made him try even harder to demonstrate his value. In 1954, he signed a contract with the Pittsburgh Pirates, the team in which he became a legend, despite the challenges he faced due to the prejudices towards his skin color and Hispanic origin. His stance on equality and respect was a lesson for the world.

During his career, Clemente won twelve "Gold Glove" awards, four "Bat Champion in the National League" titles, played in twelve consecutive All-Star games. He also won the 1966 "National League Most Valuable Player" award and the 1971 "World Series MVP" in the Fall Classic. One of the most glorious moments of his career took place in September 30, 1972. That day he connected his 3,000th hit, becoming the eleventh player to achieve this feat in the 135-year history of Major League Baseball.

In addition to being a son, brother, father, friend, and exemplary teammate, he was a leader who was always willing to help. That is the image that has remained etched in his childhood neighborhood, in Puerto Rico, and the world. Parallel to his life as an athlete and the triumphs he reaped, he never lost his humility or love for his fellow men. His concern for children and low-income communities inspired him to travel frequently to his homeland, Puerto Rico, to develop a baseball league for children. He also regularly visited Nicaragua, where he collaborated on a community project to build housing for people living in poverty. His projects were many, and his legacy is enduring.

On December 31, 1972, Roberto Clemente died while delivering provisions and humanitarian aid to the victims of the Managua earthquake in Nicaragua. The plane he was traveling on crashed into the sea, and his remains were never found. His light, however, has never been extinguished. Generations of children find in his story the inspiration they need to persevere in the pursuit of their dreams. At the same time, others see in him the example of living for the purpose of serving.

His family, friends, teachers, and those who supported Roberto had a significant impact on his growth as a person and athlete. Institutions, such as the Church, schools, and the community, also provided him the tools and knowledge to strengthen the area he valued the most: helping others. The combination of all these efforts, including the undeterred pursuit of his childhood dream, had its reward: Clemente became the first Latin American to be inducted into the Baseball Hall of Fame. Every year, the Major League Baseball organization grants the Roberto Clemente Award, reminding us that his legacy of hard work, courage, and love for our fellow men still lives strong.

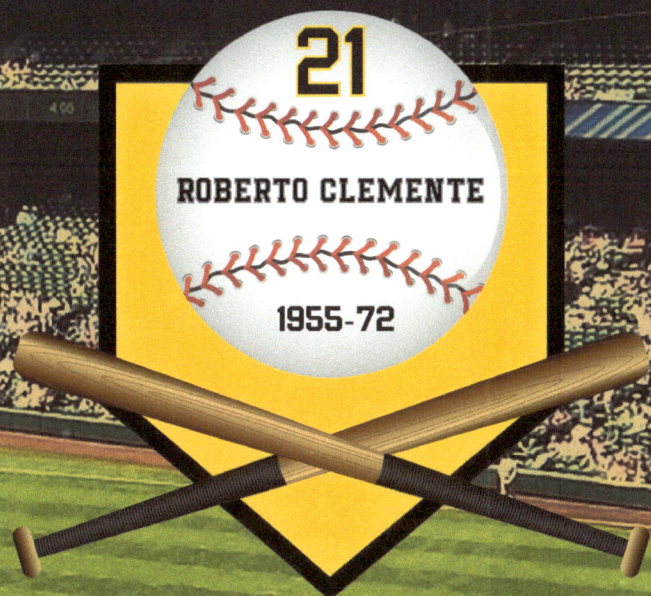

I have
VALUES

21
ROBERTO CLEMENTE
1955-72

They sowed in the heart of the world the story of a young man full of talents and love. Proving that children need to grow up under the protection of CARING PEOPLE to have real opportunities and leave a lasting legacy.

ROBERTO CLEMENTE'S Treasure Chest of Words

Self-improvement

Prejudice   Legacy

Love   Purpose

Service Significance

Discipline

Respect   Effort

Ethics   Equality

Values

ACTIVITY

#41 Read our dreamer Clemente's story and write the number of the Sustainable Development Goals addressed in each diamond.

"They say, 'Roberto, you better keep your mouth shut because they will ship you back.'
I represent the poor people. I represent the ordinary people of America.
So I am going to be treated like a human being. I want to be treated like any person who came here to work."

Roberto Clemente commenting on racism and immigration during an interview in October 1972.

Your Values

Our dreamer, Roberto Clemente, invites us to reflect on our values and principles.

Values are classified into eight categories: moral, religious, aesthetic, intellectual, affective, social, physical, and economical.

ACTIVITY

#42

Try to recall an experience of which you are very proud and satisfied with the decisions you made. Think about which values prevailed to make those decisions, write the story in your workbook and share it with whomever you wish.

Select the word from Roberto Clemente's treasure chest of words that best corresponds to each meaning in the following list:

- _____: intangible concepts and ideals that delimit each person's importance to concrete aspects of life and their relationship with their environment and people. It is subjective to every human being. They are acquired from childhood and can change throughout life.

- _____: consideration, deference, compliance.

- _____: related to maintaining order and constancy, for example, in sports and studies.

- _____: comes from the Latin *eth cus* and the Greek *êthos*, which means character. Set of moral norms that govern the conduct of a person in any aspect of life.

- _____: obligations. Equitable treatment between people. The opposite is inequality.

- _____: the action and effect of rendering a service, doing a favor, or assisting someone. Examples: public and social services.

- _____: refers to the physical force we apply against some impulse or resistance, but in a broader sense is the use of vigor, encouragement, and the will to challenge and overcome obstacles.

- _____: among its various meanings, it refers to that which goes beyond or above natural boundaries, overcoming borders or barriers.

- _____: feeling of affection, inclination, and surrender to someone or something. It is one of the most relevant values that drive a person to act for the good of others.

- _____: it is the objective, intention or desire for which an action is done or not done.

- _____: immaterial such as language, culture, example, teachings, among others.

- _____: opinion, usually of a negative nature about something or someone we do not know. It is judging before knowing (prejudging), associating without having sufficient elements, attributing something without foundations. Examples: social, ethnic, racial, religious prejudices, etc.

- _____: overcoming obstacles. The spirit of overcoming is what makes us strive to achieve our goals.

#44

My tree of values
Draw a tree on your activity workbook and write your values in it. Remember that your roots are planted in your heart.

#45

I am my own superhero
- Invent a superhero and empower them only with your values.
- Give them a name and illustrate them.
- Invent three situations where your superhero overcomes their challenges thanks to their VALUES.

IT TAKES A VILLAGE TO RAISE A CHILD
Inspired by an African proverb

#46 **THE VILLAGE OF THE CHILDREN OF THE WORLD**
With your help, many of the 2.2 billion children on
the planet will have a wonderful place
to grow, dream, and be happy.

We are counting on you!

Materials:
Poster boards, colored pencils, tempera, magazine clippings and recyclable materials. The amount and type of materials depends on your creativity.

Each dreamer from *Letter to My Dreams for the Children of the World* has shared the best part of themselves with you. And now you have many treasures to keep in your mind and your heart. Use them to serve others and become great human beings. Malala Yousafzai, Shakira, Advay Ramesh, Walt Disney, William Kamkwamba, and Roberto Clemente invite you to join them in their mission and help them build the VILLAGE OF THE CHILDREN OF THE WORLD. It is a big project. The United Nations, governments, and many organizations around the world support you and need you. There is no one better than you for this project.

Your village is unique: Let's go!

STEPS

I Be inspired by the life on our planet. Pick the place where you will build your village. Think about geography, natural resources, animals, and plants. Include everything that comes to mind you want for your village and add it to your poster board.

II Find inspiration in children. In your workbook, write a list of the children you know. Write about their needs and dreams. Use your creativity to represent on your poster board.

NAME	NEEDS	TO FULFILL THEIR NEEDS I HAVE TO...	DREAMS	TO HELP THEM REACH THEIR DREAMS I HAVE TO...
THE CHILDREN OF THE WORLD				

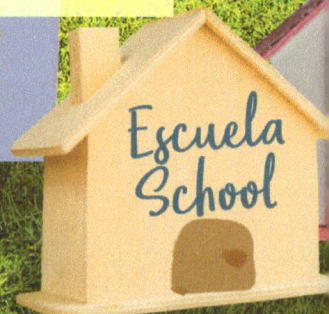

Escuela
School

THE CHILDREN OF THE WORLD

Imagine children from different parts of the world. Think about their needs and dreams. Use your creativity to represent them on your poster board.

Make sure that diversity and inclusion are part of your village. Offer the children of the world everything they need to live, be happy, and make their dreams come true.

III

Be inspired by the **17 Sustainable Development Goals of the 2030 Agenda** approved by the 193 member states of the United Nations.
• Review page **6** and make sure each goal is represented in your project.
• Review the details and think about the present and future needs.

IV   PRESENT   **THE VILLAGE OF THE CHILDREN OF THE WORLD**

The most anticipated day of the year has arrived: the presentation of your village. Share your project with your parents, friends, and teachers. Before the presentation, write in your workbook the answers to the following questions:

• Why did you choose that place to build the village, and what is so special about it?
• What do the children of that village need to live, satisfy their needs, and make their dreams come true?
• What were the challenges you faced doing this project?
• What did you learn by building the village?
• Why is it necessary for your village to meet the United Nations 17 Sustainable Development Goals?
• What does the place where you live needs to be like the village?
• What can you contribute to making the place where you live a better place?
• What did this project mean to you?

Congratulations!
You have done a great job!

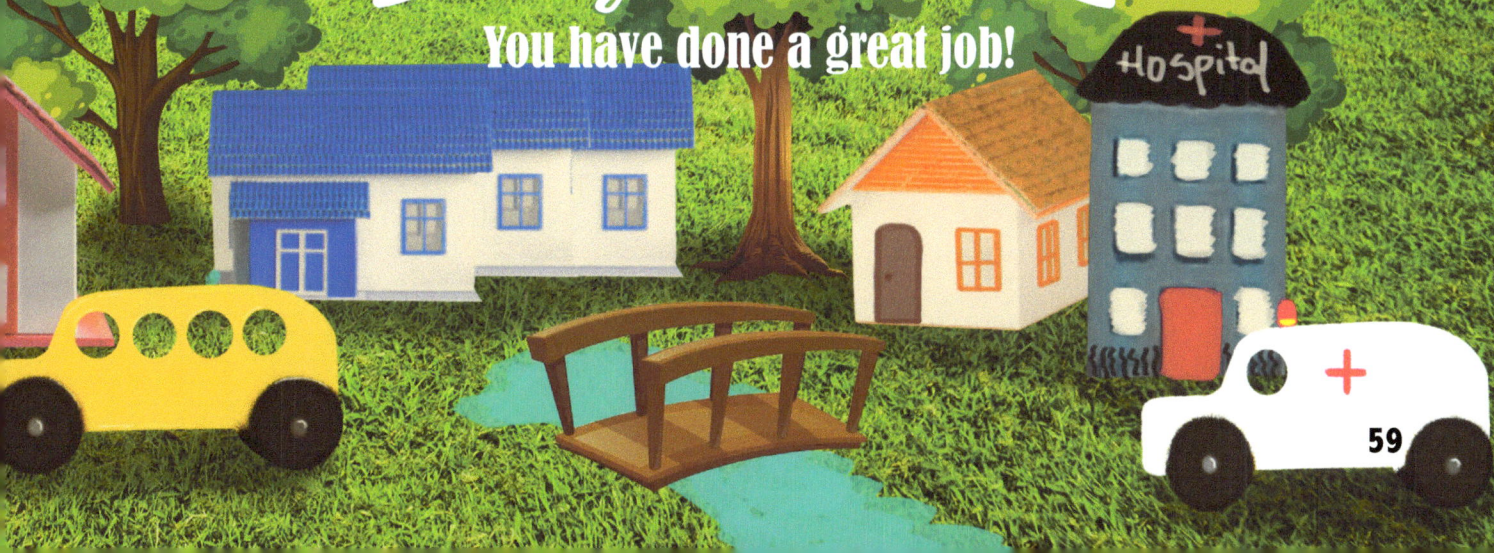

Hospital

I HAVE THE RIGHT TO

The Convention of Rights of the Child includes 54 articles about the rights of boys and girls. **You will find 10 rights we consider fundamental** to guarantee children's well-being in this list.

1. Be a child and grow up free

2. An identity and nationality

3. Health and nutrition

4. Water

5. Education

6. Have a family

7. To protection and aid

8. Not be abandoned or mistreated

9. Not be discriminated against

10. Not having to work

ACTIVITY

#47

When one has rights, one is responsible for fulfilling certain duties.

• Write a list of your duties in your workbook.

ACTIVITY #48

It is the year 2030, and the UN has invited you to represent your country with a work of art to celebrate the triumph of the 2030 Agenda. You have been asked to use recyclable material and be very original.

We are going to help you with a few easy steps:

A. Carefully read the 17 Sustainable Development Goals that appear below and think about every goal that has been achieved.

B. Write the objects or images that come to your mind when positively thinking about each goal.

1. End of poverty: _____
2. Zero hunger: _____
3. Health and well-being: _____
4. Quality education: _____
5. Gender equality: _____
6. Clean water and sanitation: _____
7. Affordable and non-polluting energy: _____
8. Decent work and economic growth: _____
9. Water, industry, innovation, and infrastructure: _____
10. Resolving inequalities: _____
11. Sustainable cities and communities: _____
12. Responsible production and consumption: _____
13. Climate action: _____
14. Underwater life: _____
15. Life of terrestrial ecosystems: _____
16. Peace, justice, and strong institutions: _____
17. Partnerships to achieve these objectives: _____

C. Using recyclable material, represent the 17 SDG and make a work of art.

D. Before traveling to the UN headquarters in New York City, United States, the president of your country has asked you to exhibit this piece at your school.
You must write on a letter-size sheet of paper the title of the work, the list of materials used, and some special detail you want to share.

E. Take a photograph of this creation and keep it as a souvenir. It was inspired by the most important project in the history of humanity, in which your support is vital.

ACTIVITY #49 — IN A GROUP:

- With your teachers' help, organize a forum at school about the importance of guaranteeing these rights.
- Did you know that children have the right to have a say?
- What happens when a child is abused?
- Why should children not work?
- Are children's rights respected?
- Who guarantees that their rights are protected?

Governments, organizations, and people around the world have joined forces to overcome these challenges:

In 2020, according to information published by the World Health Organization (WHO), about a billion children were victims of physical, psychological, or sexual violence worldwide. In most cases, these acts were not reported to the authorities.

- According to UNICEF data, children are the most affected by extreme poverty, which is the reality for more than 700 million people. "150 million more children have sunk into multidimensional poverty due to COVID-19."
- Today, nearly one billion children suffer the consequences of malnutrition and lack of drinking water.
- One in six children lives in extreme poverty.
- More than one billion children live in countries or territories affected by armed conflicts.
- Almost all deaths of children under the age of five are due to malnutrition.

There is still a lot to do!

UNICEF FOR THE CHILDREN AND ADOLESCENTS OF THE WORLD

Created in 1946 and made up of 190 countries that contribute economic resources, the **United Nations Children's Fund (UNICEF)** promotes the rights of children and adolescents, ensures their well-being, and helps them develop their potential. The fund collaborates with multiple organizations to fulfill its mission and spares no effort to help the most vulnerable and excluded children. UNICEF received the Nobel Peace Prize in 1965 for its achievements and efforts. For UNICEF, all children count.

You count!

https://www.unicef.org/

ACTIVITY #50

- Look for information about what projects UNICEF is leading to meet the goals of the 2030 Agenda for Sustainable Development for children.
- Find out if UNICEF or partner organizations exist in your country and if they are working on the goals of the 2030 Agenda.
- Mail them a card or letter introducing yourself and thanking them for their contribution to the 2030 Agenda.

You are part of the change!

IT IS TIME to write and much more!

ACTIVITY

#51

Discover the power of public speaking

You have been invited to give **a speech** on the importance of safeguarding children's welfare, including three recommendations that contribute to the well-being of children in your neighborhood.

In your workbook, write the speech using the vocabulary you have learned in *Letter to My Dreams*™ *for the Children of the World*. Read it several times aloud. Make sure you pronounce everything correctly, make the necessary pauses, have good intonation, and express what you think and feel clearly and objectively. Once you are ready, invite your parents, teachers, and classmates to listen to you. You will be surprised by the results. **Your voice is the voice of the children of the world.**

ACTIVITY

#52

Our journey does not end here:

Your speech was a success. Now you have been asked to prepare a talk for the children of the world, encouraging them to dream and persevere in their dreams. Think about possible questions they might ask and the answers, and examples of dreamers from whom they can learn. Share your dreams with them and ask them to share theirs with you.

Write your name

HAVE A DREAM FOR THE CHILDREN OF THE WORLD

ACTIVITY #54

DEAR DREAMER:

Malala Yousafzai, Walt Disney, Shakira, Advay Ramesh, William Kamkwamba, and Roberto Clemente have taught us - through their example - that we have the power to conquer our dreams and help the well-being of many people.

You are part of this great chain of dreamers that transforms the world. Many people will achieve their dreams thanks to the greatness of yours.

Invite your loved ones to write their dreams in this book...

My future

My present

I, _____
Write your name

AM A DREAMER WHO REACHED THEIR GOALS

THINK ABOUT YOUR DREAMS AND THE FUTURE. IMAGINE THE MOMENT YOU HAVE REACHED YOUR GOALS AND WRITE A LETTER TO THAT PERSON YOU WILL BECOME THE FUTURE. WHAT WOULD YOU SAY?

AFFIRMATIONS

DEAR DREAMER,

Someone once said that the longest journey one could undertake is within oneself. Today we invite you to undertake that journey and discover the wonderful being that you are. Our trip has nine affirmations inspired by our dreamers; we will visit one every day.

Are you ready?

STEPS

1

Start with Day 1.
Read the affirmation aloud.
Pause and reflect
on its meaning.
Let your heart speak!

2

Inspired by that statement,
write a letter to yourself.
Sign it, and add
the date.

3

Repeat the exercise with
the rest of the statements.
In the end, you will have 9
letters that will inspire
you for life.
Remember them always!

My dreams

DAY 1

I am the CHANGE

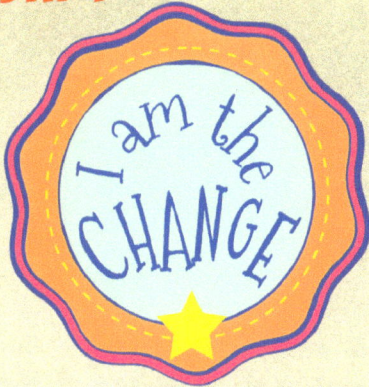

INSPIRED BY
the 17 Sustainable
Development Goals

DAY 4

I'm CREATIVE

INSPIRED BY
Walt Disney

DAY 7

I'm CLEVER

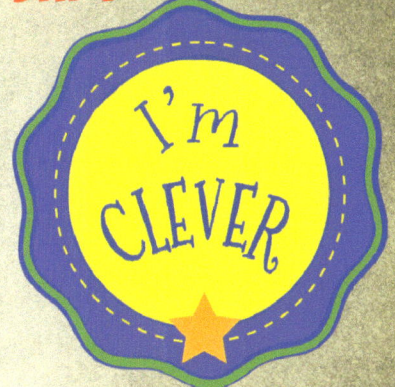

INSPIRED BY
William Kamkwamba

DAY 2

I have DREAMS

INSPIRED BY
your dreams

DAY 5

I'm ALTRUISTIC

INSPIRED BY
Shakira

DAY 8

I have VALUES

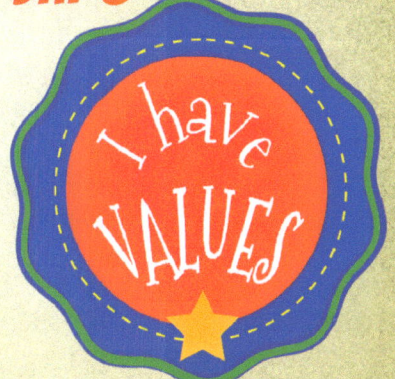

INSPIRED BY
Roberto Clemente

DAY 3

I'm BRAVE

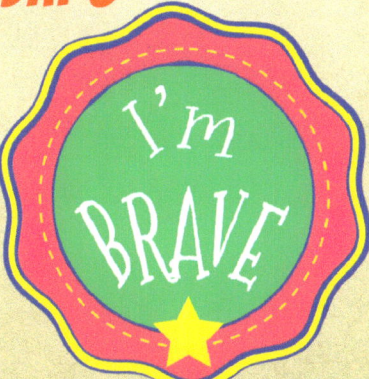

INSPIRED BY
Malala

DAY 6

I'm EMPATHIC

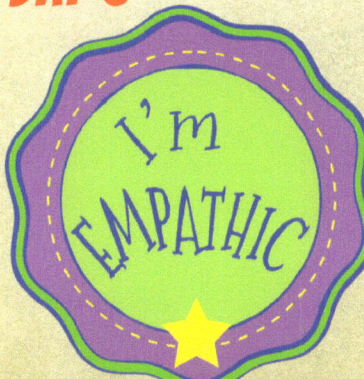

INSPIRED BY
Advay Ramesh

DAY 9

I have RIGHTS

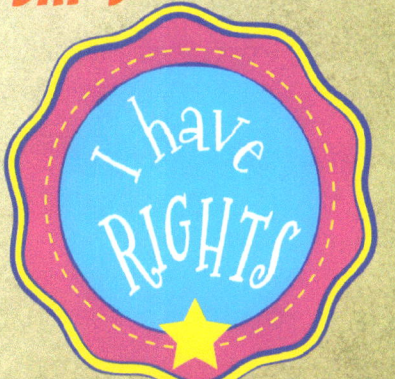

INSPIRED BY
The Rights of Children

67

Express yourself through drawings

• What I enjoy the most is...

• I would like to help...

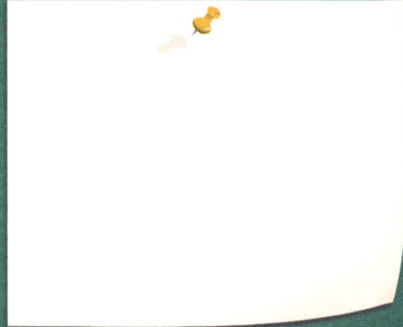

• I have 3 special treasures, and they are...

• In *Letter to My Dreams*™ for the Children of the World, I learned...

ACTIVITY #57 — **2030 AGENDA GAME**

For this game you need: 1 die, a clock, a sheet of paper and pencil, 2 Parcheesi pawns, 10 small coins and 7 seeds, for example, corn, beans, lentils, or soybeans.

Participants: 2 players or teams will represent countries A and B, and a facilitator representing the UN.

Instructions:

• The facilitator will deliver to each country: 3 coins and 2 seeds and is in charge of approving the ideas of each country to achieve the **GOALS** and overcome **situations**. The ruling is final.

• The game begins at the **START** box. The two countries must roll the dice and the one that obtains the higher score starts the game. Every time the dice is rolled, the country advances the number of boxes marked by the dice until reaching **2030 AGENDA**.

• There are no losers in this game. No country can withdraw before reaching the **2030 AGENDA** box. The country that gets there first must help the others. We will all reach the **2030 AGENDA!**

• If you want to add other players, just enlarge the columns of the streamer and draw it on a large board. **Have fun and learn!**

In this tour you will find: 17 GOALS and 12 SITUATIONS

GOALS. In each goal, you must give an idea that helps achieve said goal.

SITUATIONS. Every time a player falls into a SITUATION, they will need to offer an idea to fix the problem.

IMPORTANT. You cannot repeat the ideas or solutions that another player gave. You have a 1-minute maximum to answer.

SITUATION a
There is a drought in your country and the threat of famine. **Return to GOAL 1.**

SITUATION b
The neighboring country has an emergency and needs funds. **DONATE A COIN.**

SITUATION c
The UN gives you a coin to help you with a technological project.

SITUATION d
You must pass 2 laws, one in favor of peace and another for justice.

SITUATION e
Name two of the Rights of Children.

SITUATION f
You must create a national activity so the children in your country learn how to recycle.

START

1
2
3
4
5
6
7
8
9
10

a
b
c
d
e
f
g
h

2030 AGENDA

SITUATION g

Advance or go back to Goal 4. To advance, you must make an investment to improve education in your country.

SITUATION j

Give your neighbor a seed. If you do not have seeds, ask the UN to sell you one for two coins.

SITUATION k

You must create two sources of employment with a positive impact on reducing poverty.

SITUATION l

Think about the people who are discriminated against, and pass a law promoting equality in your country.

11
i
12
j
13
k
14
15
16
l
17

SITUATION h

Donate one coin to the UN to help in the fight against the damages to terrestrial ecosystems and marine life.

SITUATION i

Your neighboring country has an excess of food that yours needs, so they decided to exchange one coin for one seed.